Little
Blue Hut

Little
Blue Hut

Nancy Charley

Smokestack Books
1 Lake Terrace, Grewelthorpe, Ripon HG4 3BU
e-mail: info@smokestack-books.co.uk
www.smokestack-books.co.uk

ISBN 978-0-9934547-8-3

Smokestack Books is represented
by Inpress Ltd

Absorbed by change's constancy

moon rise and size, tide time and height,
shingle shift and pouting spit
patterning the waters' drift,
resident birds, transient people,
sun's arc, haze, mist and rainbows;

cirrus, cumuli cover then clear,
and with the sun, churn of waves,
a kaleidoscopic sea array

let constant change be berthed in me.

Contents

The Water-Watcher

I have assumed my watch – shifted
from southern shore of sandy beach
and rock pools under chalk cliff-face
to this northern border where the shingle
is restrained by weed-greened wooden groynes.
The horizon towards the west
is possessed by an ancient isle –
an alien ghetto I am told
where for many generations
natives lived in isolation.
And east, a strange sight, thirty spikes
spin blades – white reapers of the wind
not of the grain. The souls that fly
this coast appear as pairs of crows,
blackheaded gulls and cormorants
which dive down, stay beneath the waves
but never drown. The berths are perched
along the slope in bright array
but most are shuttered, barred and locked.
As summer slips into autumn
few seem to hear or to obey
the call to sentinel and dream.

Leaf Turner

As wanton horses cantered their churned domain

he came, crouched at the water's edge,
garnered stones to seed.

He watched the high tide turn:
an ancient one with dreadlocked hair
as oak branches when leaf-bare,
his torso and his limbs were clad
in moss and earth, grass and bark,
his face gnarled as a yew tree's trunk.

It was the day of the barley moon,
                              which rose to face the setting sun.

When the two hung opposed
he strode shingle, clambered the slope,
dropping pebbles as he trod,
clothes drying in the west wind's blasts.
As he passed I caught his scent
of leaf mould, wood smoke tinged with death.

I knew, before the night was through,
woods and fields would feel

the taint of autumn.

Shore Tales

I've heard bizarreries:

when mist purdahs the sea,
the slope rebels,
throbs with sun's kiss;

underwater bogys lurk
to graze and gash
soft swimming flesh;

merfolk rise on new moon nights
to torch the huts of foolish men
who failed to keep their bargains.

(There's evidence –
charred wood and ground,
scarred kettle and pans.)

These myths may hold validity
but there are mysteries I've seen:

bird-cones grown on the singing tree
which romance the oystermen,
then fly as sails of an old Thames barge
that trades in tales of warring days,
of shipwrecks, watchtowers and wind-tamers;

the dwellers of a clapboard cottage
pigeon cursed
aloft the wrath of the fishing firm
for encroaching upon forbidden earth;

and the martin dance along the slope,
a swooping, darting, silent homage
                              before migration.

Poppy

Crouched in the long grass on the slope,
no camouflage – this interloper's
ruddy – vivid as a sunset
on a cloudless day. She is solitary
(unlike the yellows rooted in the bay)

with yapping hounds – one black, mean, lean
whose bloodshot eyes draw you in deep
to every hell you've dreamt or seen.
The other is a scruffy, fluffy bundle
with a penchant to roll in shit
but chasing him becomes addictive.

She's here to colour your view, won't shift
before the sea sails technicolour
and bold wings unfurl on thermals.
Then she'll stand, cock a finger to the hazy
blues, browns, greys. Smile. Saunter away.

Maunsell Marksmen

Giants endure in the estuary:

On my watch I observe two clans
though once three thrived I'm told;
heroes from the warring days
with laddered legs clamped to the sea bed,
their armoured bodies held weaponry
which brought down flying enemies.

More hulk than hero now,
civvy street's been none too kind
except for three years when they ruled the waves,
pirates famed for defiant songs.

Made dumb then dumped by officialdom,
unwanted, maybe unstable,
no longer able to communicate,
the bridges between them are disintegrated.
They are reliant on the kindness of strangers
for hope in their hell.

Fey

Led by a pert, golden
        Pomeranian,
she's a flicker of pink
        that flits by the huts
in a silk ribbon dress
        puffed out by net,
strawberry-blond hair
        that glints in the sun.

I rush to seek audience
        with her queen
but fairy and familiar
        have vanished.

I retreat inside,
        stare out at the scene –
flocculent clouds
        spatter the sky
and a bistre-bice sea
        flows liltingly,
whoosh-soothe, whoosh-
        soothe, whoosh-soothe.

I'm surprised by a fragrance
        possessing my hide,
hollyhocks and heather,
        jasmine and lavender.
I begin to envision
        midsummer evenings,
woodland glens,
        small creatures feasting.

But I see the beach
        with a father and son
sporting white t-shirts,
        grey trousers and shorts,
sorting smooth pebbles
        to spin over waves.

And a dowdy frump
        who never looks up
as she traipses behind
        her mangy Alsatian.

I watch the dredger
        wend its way eastward,
depositing silt
        to replenish the seabed.

The perfume returns
        and with it the frump,
matted black hair
        disguising her features.

But my animus rises,
        sees through the mask,
flings open the door.
        I run down the slope,
welcome her majesty,
        entreat her to linger.

She smiles toothless blessing,
        continues to trudge.

The waves *whoosh* grows
        and father and son
ruffle their feathers,
        shriek and are gone.

Ancient Miners

Black as the coal which mined their lives,
Black as the dust which lined their lungs,
Black as the night which filled their days,
Black plumage, legs, feet, beaks and eyes.

Scruffily clad in workaday rags
but iridescent as sea glitter.
Restless, they scan the estuary
for barges carrying Black wealth.

They tread the shingle at tide's ebb,
eyes pick, beaks peck at each Black pebble.
They spread their wings in stunted flight.
They hop the slope with hunkered heads.

Condemned to caw when once they choired,
haunted by caged and cavernous dreams:
floods of faces, bared gleaming teeth,
laid out props, bleak Black screams.

Equinox

and on this northern shore
I prepare for the chill of being loosed
from the sun's autarchic intimacy

but ever capricious
he dazzles at the season's turn
with cirrus skies, cobalt waves,

blazons an edict to shed surplus skins,
calls the blubbered man to swim
for further cleansing.

These auguries bemuse,
do they foretell clemency
or simply lull

before a spiteful autumn.

Slope Sitters

A warm afternoon:
the incliners emerge
to flump on wooden perches,
slump in canvas nests
or sprawl upon the grass.

A quiet brood:
snooze, snuffle and snore,
tut, shush and softly babble,
ice-cream lickers, flask slurpers,
sandwich chewers, burger burpers.

Gathered flocks:
the Sun seekers face south,
Sea devotees turn north,
and worshippers of whirring vanes
mourn their loss in hazy veil.

Michaelmas Day

The market:
sparse stalls offer fruit and veg,
flowers, eggs, dusters, gadgets,
padded coats, socks and boots
(wrong-footed by unseasonal sunshine).

More curious:
a sprawl of trumpets, guitars, flutes,
salvaged brass – locks, handles, lamps,
lurid paintings, faded parasol,
boxes of wool in vivid hues.

Presided over by officers of the law
with shaded eyes and measured smiles.

Few shoppers grace this paltry scene
and there's not a goose in sight.

The harbour:
clamorous, scrabbling gulls
push and peck for prime position
atop a cockle pyramid
fed by fish-shop conveyor belt.

The reborn:
bargain battlers, market hagglers,
jumble rummagers, sales raiders,
who holidayed round charity shops
or worked in house clearance.

The Spit Sprite

The sea today
has a lulling sway in the shade of blue
that could herald a cherished son's birth

and there one glides,
grown from gutweed and hawksbeard bloom,
body bright as this Michaelmas sun,

submerged to the waist
he flicks and reels his rod and tackle,
fathoms the new moon's heightened womb.

Covering

She turns heads,
a tide of eyes enchanted by her glamour,

in shimmer of ultramarine,
          shot cobalt, crushed gunmetal,
    midnight oil splashed with glitter,
greens and browns or pinks and yellows,
      a fluidity of shades that dazzle and flux.

Her daily pilgrimage to the shore
brings murmurs of mermaid, siren or selkie.

She is none of these.

But she has sealed a pact
to watch for intruders, abusers, polluters.

Her reward:
          to stand at the flow
                              waiting
for the sea's hues to match her mood,
          then she steps down,
                    rolls in its lap,
                              slick, fast,
for the water's fickle,
flirts with sun and cloud to recast colour.

She rises, clothed,
          one of the chosen
illusion of chameleons.

How do I know?
                    Can you not guess?
From the horizon to the beach,
from the alien island to the misshapen pier
there is nothing that escapes my gaze.

Turn, see how I'm dressed.

Squall

The west wind sweeps round her thoughts.
As gulls swerve in backward flight,
as water pouts on the shore,
the west wind sweeps through her thoughts;
sifts jaundiced drifts, stillborn dawns,
salty tales, with keen insight.
The west wind sweeps up her thoughts,
gulls are swerved in backward flight.

Brink

She banters, canters,
       rumbling stones
with the booted long legs of an untrained Shire foal,

her cardigan grey
       as the morning cloud,
flaps in synchrony with her fair-flowing mane.

She views and shutters,
       teases, coerces,
rehearsing scenes with her younger sisters.

She turns, converses
       with waiting elders,
               poised

The UnSettler

He is suddenly there, feet in gloopy shallows,
hands pitted as the shingle, gaze at sea. I follow

his line of sight, he stares at surfing kites,
the arms of his jacket flap incongruously. I follow

his trudge east with steps weighty as water
at a spring tide. He paces so slowly I follow

with ease to a rendezvous with purple athlete,
a rolling guide whose glides impart energy. I follow

till they lunch, leant against the sea wall,
nibble at their whispers as they part company. I follow

past crows crowning rusted outflows,
a wetsuited woman waves at him, glares at me. I follow

his semaphore, decipher the message,
a murmuration of starlings in ascendency. I follow

as he tears at marram grass and glasswort,
misery mirrored in deserting sea. I follow

colour shift: sallow sunset, black clouds stacking
cause a sea change from dull to lucency. I follow

but I cannot unriddle who he might be,
whether his presence alters Water-Watcher's destiny.

A Song of Hibernation

I wrapped my heart in a cotton shroud,
I wound my heart in a silk cocoon,
I gave my heart to the carrion crows
who flew my heart to a lace day moon.

The moon sank into a bruise-tinged haze,
my heart slipped into the cold cold waves.
The current twisting from flow to ebb
carried my heart away   away.

I trapped my sorrow behind panes of glass,
I hid my body in a pinewood shed,
I pooled my tears for marygold drink,
I stifled my sobs in spider webs.

But a money-spinner comforted me,
crawled my hand as I scrawled my hurt,
taught my lament to the screaming gulls,
scattered my anguish to pecking culvers.

I will bathe my face in the morning dew,
I will pinch off fear to feed crane flies,
I will sprinkle self-pity along the shingle,
skimming pebbles as anger dives.

My skin will absorb a radiant sunset,
my body will bask in crepuscular rays,
I will wade in the shallows when cats' paws thrill,
I will dance with the moon's corona display.

My heart will return when autumn is dead,
once winter is sifted and spring has sprung,
my heart will stir in its shrouding cocoon,
bloody my body, release my tongue.

My heart will return as a cormorant
lumbering silently over the sea,
oiled and preened and cruciate,
embracing others and saving me.

Gutting

On moon-shy nights wrapped in swirling sea fret,
when black waves welter with unbridled rage,
they rise to bore holes in cargo-boat holds
and sabotage foreigners to their coast.
Next day, they arrive in the harbour – bold
men with diving gear and mouths full of boasts
of expertise in retrieving salvage,
for a fee they'll fetch bounty from the wreck.
But it's said no-one's sure how much is saved,
they hide the truth about the plunder raised.
This story exposes these gutweed sprites
who must be underwater by twilight
or stay condemned to search the shore each dusk
with trowel, muffled ears and sweeping trudge.

The Fisher

He's clothed to sway the sea today,
dull blue and brown with hints of grey.
He's angling for her to bestow
creaturely favour, so he'll know
the bounty held beneath her swathes.

Facing the groyne he kneels to pray,
rises to cast into the waves.
Impotent, he must wait, although
he's clothed to sway.

A pull, he reels in straightaway
but finds in faith there is betrayal.
With seaweed tangled line she shows
floundering rites cause her sorrow.
Impenetrable, though arrayed
in clothes that sway.

Initiation

The setting sun splits a cloud-pitched sky
and charms the sea to sparkle blue
as a scrum of youths, with uniformed flanks, weave
and pass, an elder coaches at the back.
Eight strip and plunge to tackle ring-o-roses,
submerge their nerves, exuberant emerge
to line-out on the shingle, drink bottles
of potent elixir, spin-dizzy-sick-spin-dizzy-sick.

An uphill struggle to try their mettle:
bare-chests barefoot one third race, retrace
gained ground; two thirds run and turned
around; a doddery jog to the top, where
they are felled; odd-shaped balls tumble down.
Those who stand receive their stripes, clasp
shaking hands convinced of their conversion.

Light House

The full moon is hidden by heavy cloud
but *Beacon House* heads the ebb-tide spit

with rays that change coniferous branches
to luciferous, tousled tresses

and a facade that is recast
as a premature Halloween mask.

A Day of Pairs

Where have you come from plump country folk,
all bluster and fuss, trussed in Sunday-best tweeds,
strutting the slope, ignoring the sea?

We flew from the woods to visit the market,
we're pecking away at our disappointment,
the lack of wild oats or golden corn seed.

Where are you going craggy, wise hags,
one dressed with sky, one clothed with the land,
mouths filled with gossip, hands filled with bags?

We've stashed secrets to spill to the wind,
trading our wisdom for inspiration
to ramble until the end of our path.

Why stand motionless well-weathered spouses
with gazes opposed, feet planted in shingle,
shoulder-to-shoulder in silent communion?

We wait for a signal to face the sea,
toss bread on the waters, take leave of the beach,
our synchronised steps in time with our dreams.

Why do you stride, measured and fast
to the guards' hut and back, lean bodies held taut,
uniformed in black with cap, wide-brimmed hat?

This is the time of the morning lesson,
by my coat's orange lining you'll know my business
and this red-chest weasel is my apprentice.

Why are you perched in witches' cloaks,
oily and preened on your scarlet outpost?
Why double when usually solitary?

We come and go to no-one's command,
we dive through the waves, dry out on the land,
how many you see is illusory.

Why walk alone morose young man,
grey parka and boots, beige hat and bag,
hands thrust in pockets and pensive slouch?

He gave no reply, lost to his mood,
but the shrouding clouds followed his route
and a sombre sky was loosed to be blue.

Glimpses

All day a jubilant sun
chases a sliver of moon.

A Turneresque haze
playing with water colours
hides the horizon.

The advancing, chanting sea
dances with the shingle's beat.

Two swimmers appear
as aberrant white horses
foaming the water.

Retired jacketed greyhounds
jog with jacketed owners.

A breeze thieves the time,
three aging dandelions
loosen their fleeces.

Single file, synchronised flap
towards sunset, geese fly past.

Sea Weeds

Daily she gathers armfuls of bladderwrack, carries them home,
dries until black, then weaves fronded weeds for her love.

Yet she fetches sea lettuce and gutweed to feed on their juices,
resourcing strength, awaiting the dawn of mourning's end.

Ruddy Ruse

Last night's hidden harvest moon aroused suspicion.
So though today is bright, blue sky laced with white,

      anxiety clouds. I weave

towards the harbour mouth, its jaws adorned
with worn tractor tyres, so my thoughts turn

to ploughing, sowing, hoping crops are harvested.
Tuc-tuc-tuc splits

           my reverie, *tuc-tuc-tuc.*

Black and white stripes flash past in flurried fright
their shadows pointing to a full moon cast

upon the shingle. Turn stone alchemy –
ochre, grey, sienna, black veined or speckled –

      all blood red.

And at the groyne's end an apple gleams
rich as the autumn sun. What glamour.

My lips twitch, mouth drools.
I pick.
         Trk-it-it-it

Turnstones save. I toss the fruit to the waves.
Whoosh-no, whoosh-no, a churning sea returns it.

I know the spell:

Build a pyre of blood-stones. Set
fire. Waft the smoke to east and
west. Stoke. Watch. Wait. Make
sure no core remains. Souse
with sea to cleanse the beach.
Bury every reddened pebble in a
pit dug deep.

Birds settle on the harbour wall but I'm disturbed
by what manner of enchantment we have turned.

The OtherWise

Just before noon

the autumnal wych-elm wolf prowls,
white tail held down in peace

Summons seven to chatter and chant

one conjures haze to obscure the giants
all come laden with tasty morsels

one casts a line to reel in a spit sprite
all sip from flasks, quaff from flagons

one sets ten virgins to sail on blue water
all settle in, exchanging viewpoints

one turns swimmers to foaming horses
all pick and poke at the treasures I've hoarded

one sends birds to unfurl the barge
all pay homage to sea and sky

one magics models with their photographer
all embrace a myriad shifting shapes

one weaves silk from spider thread
all are bellyful with feast and laughter

At afternoon's end

they leave as geese in flight
head toward the alien island

Rising

This is the day the sea lost its sway.
> *This day the clouds held control over hue,*
as hanging low, they leached colour away.

> The day began as a man in black
with skipping ropes and twirling batons
> stood on the shingle sending signals.

This day accumulated cumuli,
> *mountain high, turned water grey*
but cotton bud scud bestowed yellow-green waves.

> The morning filled with grass-cutters,
a drone that swelled with roused insects,
> a starling racket flown in to lunch.

At noon, as clouds cleared in the west,
> *the sea two-toned in blue and charcoal,*
cut by a line from shore to horizon

> which brought the man in the motorised chair,
caped and cowled, dressed for prayer,
> with pilgrim pups knelt in his basket.

Bewitchment came as a skein of geese

> opened an aperture in the sea.
I will not disclose the face
> or form of the one who rose.

But his breath becoming breeze
> *resigned this sentinel to leaving.*

Animation

I remember the woman wrapped in coat, swaddling towel
who waddled the slope an hour before sundown.

She slid on the shingle, clattering pebbles against the groyne,
enchanted five stones to skim through the foam.

She shed her apparel and waded in,
ankles, calves, thighs flushing at water's sting.

Lithely she ducked into the lapping caress,
hands twirling, arms swirling with intricate grace,

her curly-haired head like a plumped bobbing gull,
she swivelled and swayed, embracing, lulled.

I remember how her lilting songs crescendoed
the *whoosh-shirr* percussion, the peace as she ended.

Passersby, in their hurry, fleetingly stared,
muttered, *No sense. Must be nutty,* but she didn't care

for this was escape from humdrum housewife,
wombed by the water, tingling alive.

The Harbour Harridan

Bind lobster pincers.
Bed on bladderwrack.
Wrap in flame and
name your enemy to
trap them in your grasp

She knows the spell,
        finds her name in charred remains.

She had watched an inky sky turn pink,
        clouds tinge gold, a sienna dawn.

She had risen for blessing,
        fallen on curse.

She beseeches the presiding Great Blackback,
        sacrifices cockles upon driftwood.

Goo-go-go
        He screeches unmoved.

She stumbles on the shingle,
        her rasp summons carrion crows.

October New Moon's Eve

The day dawns with drumming rain
and throughout the day storm clouds hover
so sun and showers fight for dominance.
Today I must vacate this place,
end my watch on the northern shore,
a day to pack and ponder.

I stand and stare at the sea's blue shimmer,
tinged with turquoise, fleckled brown,
intermittent metallic slicks.
The tide flows quiet, quiet, quiet
so all I hear is a plane's dull drone
and *caw caw caw* of the slope's two crows.

I've stood watch for forty-five days,
watched this autumn entranced by sun.
I began at full moon, end at new.
Like me, the sea's a chameleon,
I've watched through countless colour shifts
as if survival depends on this.

I've seen sea sparkle, seen it drab,
seen the sea sliced by cloud and sun –
half greeny-grey, half cobalt sheen.
I've seen hue leached by low cloud cover,
seen the sea transform to a pastel emulsion
fit for the room of a newborn son.

The sunset paints with pink and orange,
throws the water a golden orb,
daubs the horizon scarlet and purple.
I've seen sea sky become one blur,
seen a black inkwell at dead of night
haunted by red, green, amber lights.

Sunrise, sunset are sinking south
as light-blessed hours daily dwindle.
I've marked stone drift along the beach,
seen a muslin moon fall in the sea.
I've walked the spit at lowest ebb,
seen ancient rites, alchemy.

I've watched gulls – herring, great black-backed,
black-headed feathered winter white.
I've been engrossed by cormorants,
by the flurry of turnstone flight,
by the skurry of oyster catchers,
by passing flocks of geese and swallows.

Though I was sent as sentinel
it is apprentice I've become
to weed and shingle, wind and sun,
to clouds and birds, tide and moon
but most of all to shade and hue.

Little Blue Hut

'A wasting woman is wasted wealth.'

Begotten of the moon, formed by the sea,
birthed with the earth, we genii three
are covenanted sisters bound to agree.

~   ~   ~

One bleak winter snow cradled the ground,
like fondant icing on a celebration cake,
and in the north a baby was born

(but no party held). As the youngest of five
she had to fit with her mother's routine,
her father's short shrift.

When the child was seven they uprooted,
settled on the midlands in a bungalow
set in the middle of an orchard.

But the apples were tart and maggoty.
She learnt to peel, slice and core,
eat once stewed.

It was her father's chore
to pick the apples, she plucked plums
that hung on a twisted tree.

With each passing year this girl grew –
her body grew tall, her hair grew straggly,
her teeth grew crooked (the dentist embraced them)

and her head grew full of questions.
But her mother was busy,
father unforthcoming,

so the questions jittered
                inside her mind
without answers.

Her sisters and brothers, each in turn,
left the family home to study and work.
The girl's chance came,

                she ventured north
hoping to gather her answers.
Instead she reaped a crop of friends

who chatted and partied,
                prattled and danced.
And a handsome man romanced her.

She bundled her questions into recesses,
married the man and as time
trundled on

mothered four children. Her mind filled
with their joys and troubles,
                her heart filled

with their love and laughter,
                her life filled
with chores and toys and childish adventures.

~   ~   ~

We weave ribbons, these braided strands
will whip her night-mares, tie her hands
till she resolves to seek this land.

~   ~   ~

'Why no joy in mending and knitting,
    in tending my garden,
       in cleaning and baking?

Why no joy in tattling with neighbours?
My children fly yet I stay tied.
My routine's outlived its helpful life.

Why dream upon dream of barren fields
where starlings *schrien,*
                peck, peck, peck;

of tumbling through quiescent seas
unable to float, unable to drown;
of stumbling down bramble-strewn paths

on nights when the moon has lost her glow;
of echoes:
   Luna

              Marina

                          Hertha'

~   ~   ~

Helga, Cracus, fly from your lair.
A famished woman feasts on despair.
May your black presences nourish care.

~   ~   ~

'Shadowy figures
       banish hope with cackling fury.
They swoop and strut with flapping cloaks,

stirring, stirring. Beckon me
with six-fingered hands. All week
two crows have commandeered my bird-feeder.'

~   ~   ~

A woman travails for hidden sight.
Moon, compel her to treasure your light,
to follow the corvids in homeward flight.

~   ~   ~

The birds seemed set to peck all her seed
but their restless hop-
                              hunker perturbed.

They flew to saplings
                    that bordered the garden
each time she stepped out.

Kraaa-kraaa-kraaa discorded taut nerves.
She must leave.
                    Fly where crows lead.

She stuffed a backpack with clothes and food,
found a storm-proof coat, her stoutest shoes,
whittled a stick from a fallen oak branch.

Wanting to flee with her neighbours asleep
she opened her door one late summer's evening.
Countless stars glittered but no moon shone.

                    The crows were gone.
Distraught she sought through streets, in the park,
recklessly croaking *kraaa-kraaa-kraaa.*

A myriad creaks, rustles and shrieks
left dark shadows.
                    No crows.

She searched till dawn, stumbled on home,
hope pecked apart. Nested in bed,
          she wept.

Foetal, she curled that day and the next,
unable to rise to her normal routine.
In fitful sleep on the third afternoon

Kraaa
                    Silence.
She buried her head in the pillow.

Kraaa
                              Kraaa
            Kraaa-kraaa

From her window she glimpsed
a lace-moon sliver
                    and two crows.

She grabbed clothes, hurriedly dressed,
slung on her backpack, picked up her stick,
flung open the door half-expecting to find

crows vanished.
                    Instead they circled twice
round her head, flew off down the road.

No longer caring if neighbours saw,
she slammed the door
                    and followed.

        ~   ~   ~

Wind, be still. Weather, stay fair.
A woman walks within our snare.
The Little Blue Hut we will prepare.

        ~   ~   ~

'I journey south
 caught in some corvid master-plan.
 Each day crow rise grows later.

They're hard to track
            on cloud-black nights,
trusting *kraaa-kraaa* to direct my path.

I've tripped over tree roots,
                    fallen in ditches.
I am bruised and scratched

but stars propel me,
moon coronas circle my pleasure.
I have walked from evenings

                        into nights
through to mornings. It has been four weeks.
I long to continue but the crows are gone.'

            ~   ~   ~

When a crescent moon beguiled the sky,
the crows reappeared, continued to fly
                    south-east.

At last they came to a shingle beach.
The woman, exhausted, lay down and slept,
woke at sunset.

            ~   ~   ~

'A golden sun slipping to the sea
splashes the clouds buttercup and rose,
casts a haze of blues and mauve,

shimmers sea silver.
A cream barley-moon climbs a pewter sky.
I shiver, zip up my storm-proof coat.

Kraaa-kraaa, kraaa-kraaa.
                    Crows startle.
On a moonlit slope they strut

towards a small hut.
A wood-pigeon waddles, keys in beak,
drops them at my feet.

I enter the darkness of the hut,
                    lie starry-eyed
until sleep overcomes.'

            ~   ~   ~

She is here
            she is here
                        she is here

By scourge of shingle and tussle of tide,
each sister will be inquisitor and guide,
raid recesses for treasure that hides.

Luna   Luna   Luna
    lull   lift   lustrate
        lavish   lace   illuminate

            ~   ~   ~

'Waves wreck my dreams,
creatures scream, hurl shingle,
flurry in flight.

                After such a night,
I wake aching. The hut is dark
but a shaft of light leaks under the door.

I take down the shutters and daylight floods
over table and chairs,
                rug, blankets and cushions.

A single shelf holds bottles and jars,
baskets and packets, and on one wall
a mirror hangs.

               I refrain from looking,
drawn to the photo of a blazing grotter.
Flames lick my mind.

                 I dash outside.
Who owns this place? Why am I here?
Excitement jiggles with hope and fear.'

      ~   ~   ~

She watched the sky, she watched the sea,
saw day spread to night, tides flow and ebb.
She watched kites dance,

               tangle strings,
shadows foretell their owners' appearing,
how the scene changed if she glanced away.

She scuffed shingle, noticed each pebble's difference
and that she felt much lighter
free from her backpack's weight.

She avoided the mirror's call,
afraid of the image
            she fleetingly saw.

A spider weaved in one corner.
She resisted the urge to brush it aside,
relinquished a thread of domestic pride.

On the seventh day she found a standpipe,
filled bowl after bowl,
strip-washed, scrubbed at her clothes.

With scissors in hand she decided to face
the mirror. Snipping at her overgrown hair,
she was suddenly aware

       someone was there.
Turned.
          No-one.

    ~   ~   ~

'I wake on the eighth day
to a cloud-free sky,
several women jog by.

I itch to stretch strengthened legs.
I open the door. A half-moon hangs.
There she is,

        the mirror image,
white-muslin gowned from chin to feet,
silver-tinged hair.

Do you know?

Do I know why I'm here?
Do I know where here is? Do I know
what will happen? Do I know who she is?

A dozen questions flood my mind
but I am dumb,
awed by stony eyes and gravelly tone.

Do you?

Do I miss my home? Do I want
more? Do I care for life?
Do I dare search further?

Will you walk with me?
                              I nod.
All morning along the shore

she questions, questions in her grave voice.
Then she is gone. I am alone
with memories stirred of a straggly-haired girl.

Next morning she's there
when I open the door and the next,
the next, the next.

Every day
her voice sharpens, her body wizens,
questions penetrate

                              as icy daggers.
I am scared and fascinated in equal measure.
Who is she?

I see the questions in your mind.
I see patience restrain curiosity's flight.
I am Luna, one of three.

I leave. You must seek my ribbon.
Be bound to this task and you'll discover
allies who will draw you closer.

'How can I find… How can I know…?'

My ribbon is white or silver or gold.
Don't be surprised by what you behold.
But beware. Some will try to tie you.

'How can I…?'

Not how but who. By heart and eyes.
Complete the task before I rise
with Marina, my sister.'

~　　　　~　　　　~

All day she pondered Luna's request.
That night she dreamt of thimbles and threads,
of pedlars, parties and maypole dances,

of ribbons switching to dragons' tongues
which grew bodies, gave her chase.
She woke heart thumping and breathless.

Upbraiding herself,
she set off on her task.
                        She asked

wind-surfers and swimmers,
sunbathers and skimmers
drawn by the sun's clemency

but their advice was contradictory.
None the wiser she lapped up
their chat, glad of company.

~　　　　~　　　　~

By crow craw and gull screech,
this woman must cease her idle speech.
Helga, Cracus, deny her the beach.

~　　　　~　　　　~

'I dreamt of crows plucking at clothes.
I opened the hut door, they flew at my face.
I swatted and swished

                        but they persist.
I retreat inside. I miss
            new friends. I'm lonely.

If I'd never embarked on this journey
I could be gossiping with my neighbours,
I could be about my daily business.'

~   ~   ~

Kept inside,
                she fretted and fumed,
relived her life through all its downturns.

But in her dreams a young girl sought
chalk-face caves and the afternoon's
                                new moon.

~   ~   ~

'I must go to the harbour.
'*Please crows,
release me from the hut.*"

~   ~   ~

Crows flew, she followed,
resisted the *whoosh* of sea on shingle,
beached people calling.

She searched not knowing what she should find:
a life-ring, dried seaweed, lobster claws,
a weatherboard shed

shuttered and locked, the remains of a fire.
A flock of turnstones flustered by,
settled on the harbour wall.

She turned to the sea's soothing rhythm
but shrill notes disturbed her musing –
                                a choir

dressed in chestnut cloaks, white skirts, orange boots,
twittered: *You came west*
                              Go back east

Keep to the shore
                        By haggling gaggle
You will know more.

She blinked. Turnstones took flight,
black and white stripes patterned the sky
and on the breeze a staccato song:

Tuc-tuc-tuc
            Speed-speed-speed
                              Their presence is brief.

She walked east seeking clues.
A skein of Brent geese flew overhead,
landed at a distant shingle bay.

As she approached, the beach became a market.
Stall-holders, wearing black jackets, white aprons,
croaked and shouted: *Will you buy?*

'I need help.'   *Will you haggle?*
'With what?'   *What have you got?*
'Nothing.'   *You bring nothing?*

'What do you want?'   *Are you asking?*
'Am I asking?'   *Are you haggling?*
'With a question?'   *For me?*

'Who are you?'   *Who are you?*
'What do you want?'   *What do you want?*
'To find Luna's ribbon.'   *Find what your heart longs for…*

With a croak and a *krutt* the market was gone.
The flowing tide lapped at her feet.
She stumbled up the beach.

~   ~   ~

'I have paced east and west.
I seem no further forward. I must rest.
I will return to the Little Blue Hut.'

~   ~   ~

She walked towards the setting sun.
Near to the hut she stopped, entranced
by a cormorant on a high post.

She watched as the bird oiled and preened,
spread its wings, dived into the sea,
surfaced with a shining eel in its beak.

As she turned to climb the slope,
                    she was cloaked,
then released. A man knelt

at her feet – black cape, top hat.
By sleight of hand he produced
a silver ribbon from his throat.

Luna is pleased that you can obey.
This ribbon is yours if you can say
three things that wax and wane.

'The first is the moon. I know her journey
through the sky. The second is the tide.
It ebbs and flows and by moon's

pull, lessens and grows in its surge.'
Well done. One more?
'I'm not sure…'

Trust what your heart longs for.
The woman's thoughts dredged through fear
and into her mind came a straggling teenager

with so many questions.
'A woman?'
>   *The ribbon is yours.*

~   ~   ~

By mensal charm, curse is reversed.
But too-tame woman stays rehearsed
in rules and hurts since childhood nursed.

By whip of kelp and churn of waves,
Marina, unleash wildish ways,
erode maternal masquerades.

~   ~   ~

'Two women approach –
one young, radiant, with straw-blond hair,
one dreadlocked and haggish

but the dress she wears
shimmers and shifts with each step she takes.
Don't be surprised.

Who are these? Luna? Marina?
Swim with me. Her voice ripples,
>   drips into my mind.

Swim with me.
Marina splashes in the shallows
>   *Swim with me.*

I shake my head. 'My mother said…'
>   *Swim with me.*
Waist deep, her voice ripples and rings.

I look for Luna, needing approval.
She's gone.   *Swim with me.*
I plant my feet on the shingle.

'My mother insisted the sea is dangerous –
tangling weed, stinging creatures,
hidden currents, sewage outlets, and...'

Only her head bobs above
the water.
> *Swim with me, daughter.*

The ribbon I hold is turning gold.
I tie back my hair, slip from my shoes,
enter the sea.

>   She glides with ease. I struggle,
each incoming wave tosses me.
I gulp in mouthfuls of salty water

as time and again I'm pulled under.
I find her on a granite rock.
She hauls me up.

	Strip off your clothes.
'I can't do that.'	*Strip off your clothes.*
'I'll be exposed.'	*Strip off*

Nails like knives
>   she rips clothes to ribbons.
These are not the ribbons you need.

Feel wind and spray.
>   *Fly.*
Scavenge with Great Blackback.'

    ~   ~   ~

A shadow fell. The woman shivered.
A powerful gull, black wings tipped white,
soared overhead, its yellow bill

screaming: *Goo-go-go*
Dare   Stretch out
                              Soar

The woman timidly unclasped her arms.
She grew feathers of mottled black-brown
and her mouth became a flesh-coloured beak.

                              She shrieked
but she and her protestations were caught
by the wind   to fly.

 Flying was tricky. She had to tilt wings
 to find the wind's thrust,
                    use its lift to carry her up.

So often she plummeted
                    into the water.
The Great Blackback aimed for cliffs,

                    swooped to plunder
other birds' nests, dashed chicks against rocks.
Appalled she watched.

                    You-you-you.
'I can't kill.'   *Feed-feed-feed.*
'I would rather die.'   *Die-die-die.*

Feeling faint she began to fall
towards the cliffs. She felt torn.
Her 'sorry' erupted as an awful screech.

She grabbed a chick, pulverised it,
swallowed flesh and bone.
                    Done-done-done.

Goo-go-go.   Great Blackback soared high.
The woman returned to nakedness,
tried to hide as Marina arrived.

Death in life, life in death
release the questions that stifle breath.
Come, there is more to be done.

They dived
into the water, stroke by stroke
they swam together.

On the shore a crowd was massed,
clothed in white and black with long pink boots,
eyes and mouths burnished orangey-red.

'Who are they?'   *Come, they are waiting.*
'I can't leave the water.'   *They are waiting.*
'I have no clothes.'   *They will not wait long.*

Even as she protested
the crowd stirred, murmured restlessly.
Lose to gain.

The woman rose from the water.
Immediately she was engulfed by chat.
Embarrassed, stuttering, she wondered why

no-one mentioned her nudity. Were they blind?
But she was magnetised by strange conversations,
stimulating, illuminating, capricious,

which drew from the woman unspoken ideas,
questioned her questions,
threw plans in the air.

A flurry of wings. They were gone.
Oystercatchers flying into the sun.
Marina stood naked, her dress in her hands.

                                   For you.
'I will be different.'   *Yes.*
'I can't take what is yours.'   *The sea clothes me.*

The woman walked towards the sunset –

sea and sky were bathed saffron and gold,
flamingo and flame, tangerine and carmine
and the haze bruised rose and gun-grey.

She stopped to gaze, utterly absorbed
but glancing down discovered her dress
was ripple and sheen, reflecting the scene.

As she climbed the hut's steps in the gloaming,
the woman slipped, touched slime and screamed.
She picked up kelp, which in her hands

transformed to a ribbon of marled green-brown velvet.

~   ~   ~

A wistful woman wastes precious minutes.
By hog's fennel and rock pipits
redefine her precious limits.

Hertha

        Hertha

                Hertha

harness

        heal her

                birth her

~   ~   ~

'I'm startled awake as the door's flung wide,
the daylight is blocked by a bosomy woman
bedecked with baskets and a long-handled broom.

If you wouldn't mind rubbing the sleep from your eyes,
I think you will find some have work to do.
She starts to unpack, replenish stocks.

I am Hertha. I knew you'd be asking.
And you won't mind me saying this hut is a mess,
so you should dress,

                      make yourself scarce…
'Sorry, I wasn't expecting a guest.'
I'm no guest. Off you go.

'I could help…'
No, you could not. Times and seasons.
She shoos me to the door, tosses a basket.

Find me elderflowers,
               sea asparagus,
                          wild strawberries.

All day I search
but cannot find what she requested.
My spirits sink with the setting sun.

I head to the hut, hoping she's gone
but she's spread-eagled across the grass,
tatting a rug. *Ah, you're back. No luck?*

'No…'
I realise her attention is held elsewhere.
I follow her gaze. A gaggle of geese

                          fly east.
'A wild goose chase.'
Exactly. Times and seasons.

In clothes of russet and auburn
               I embrace autumn
like those black-headed gulls.

She points to the shingle where the gulls
squawk, squabble, chase and flap.
Their heads are white with a single black dot.

'There are no black heads.'
Exactly. Times and seasons.
Why don't you join them?'

~   ~   ~

Shooed off again, the woman plodded the slope,
wearily wondering, why bother with birds?
Her eyelids drooped,

she paused for a moment.
Her nostrils caught the aroma of wood smoke.
She opened her eyes to a roaring bonfire

where white-garbed women,
wrapped in grey blankets,
sat chatting, happily cackling.

She entered their circle.
A feisty woman started to sing.
They all joined in:

A January baby will never be a lady,
She always squirts her shit
if her father's nappy-changing.
Oh, raise your voices, lasses
and squeal, shriek, screech.

A February child is never meek and mild,
By splattering her dinner
she sends babysitters wild.
Oh, sing for supper, lasses
and squeal, shriek, screech.

A March girl has one sin, dear, to love a reckless shindig,
And one thing else is sure, dear,
March is always windy.
Oh, lift your skirts, lasses
and squeal, shriek, screech.

In April don't be fooled by a maiden acting cool,
She's plotting how to swerve
                    from her father's made-up rules.
Oh, blot your lipstick, lasses
                    and squeal, shriek, screech.

In May you would be crazy to ever trust a lady
Who saunters down the street
                    with a basketful of daisies.
Oh, pick petunias, lasses
                    and squeal, shriek, screech.

A red rose in June will find you bleeding soon,
Watch for the thorny stem, sir,
                    you'll never be a groom.
Oh, toast with red wine, lasses
                    and squeal, shriek, screech.

A heat-wave in July gives us ample reasons why
to be at one with nature,
                    if it rains we'll tumble dry.
Oh, strip the willow, lasses
                    and squeal, shriek, screech.

A cloud-free August day is the time for making hay,
Fields waiting to be harvested,
                    we shall not waste today.
Oh, swing your scythes, lasses
                    and squeal, shriek, screech.

The apples in September are crisp and very tender,
For one juicy bite, girls,
                    fortunes are surrendered.
Oh, stir the pudding, lasses
                    and squeal, shriek, screech.

And now we're in October, our song is nearly over,
But we are in our prime, girls,
                    for rolling in the clover.
Oh, seize the day, lasses
                    and squeal, shriek, screech.

The women erupted in raucous laughter.
A herring gull swooped,
circled twice and as its feet touched down

there stood a lady in full white gown,
black and white tassels fringing her grey shawl.
Silence fell.

I've a tale to tell if you've bread and wine.
Food and drink given, the women settled
and the story began:

Once long ago, in a land faraway, there lived a wise woman. She'd raised three kind sons and two fine-skilled daughters and for that she was respected. But the woman didn't realise she was wise. So when a lass, expecting her first child, asked, 'What shall I do when the baby cries?' The woman replied, 'My dear, I really don't know. Maybe try feeding, winding or cuddling. Perhaps push in its pram or play peek-a-boo. Maybe just leave it to cry.' The girl did all the woman had suggested. The baby thrived, bonny and contented.

A widow asked, 'How can I survive?' The woman replied, 'My dear, I really don't know. I'm sure that selling vegetables, taking in ironing or knitting mittens ready for the winter wouldn't help much.' The widow tried the woman's ideas, earned enough to stay housed and fed.

And so it went on. Each time she was asked for a piece of advice, she replied, 'Well, my dear, I really don't know...', then made some suggestions which were always helpful. But the woman felt useless with her children grown, no-one to care for at home.

One day a blind man walked down her street, tapping his stick as he stumbled along. 'Oh dear,' thought the woman, 'that man needs helping.'

She stepped out from her house. 'Good day to you, sir. I see you can't see. Shall I walk with you a while, be your eyes?'

'It would bring me pleasure to have your company. But I have eyes that work just fine,' the man replied. 'I can see Mrs Greedhog has roast pork again, Mr Mowlawn has his garden in order and that Johnny Sweetface has been chewing toffee.'

'Your telling is true. How do you see?'

'I see with my nose, my ears and my hands. I see with my heart and my mind. And by my seeing I can tell that I talk with a wise woman.'

'Wise woman? That's not me.'

'My telling is true.'

And with a twirl of his white walking stick and three harsh shrieks, he was gone.

And with flap of wings the storyteller vanished.
'Your turn. Yessss', hissed the circle.
The woman was pushed to her feet.

'Sing of the shifting dress you wear,
tell of the ribbons in your hair.'
She blushed and stuttered, finally said,

'You have all been so welcoming
but I'm afraid, I really don't know…'
It was many minutes before their laughter subsided

but in that time inspiration came. She began:
Sssshh-ssshh-ssshh-ssshh, ssshh-ssshh,
Ssshh-ssshh-ssshh-ssshh, ssshh-ssshh.

Some joined in quietly.
Once she was sure they knew rhythm and tune,
she changed her refrain:

Splash-dash-dash, Splash-dash-dash, Sprittle and whirr,
Splash-dash-dash, Splash-dash-dash, Sprittle and whirr,
Splash-dash-dash, Splash-dash-dash, Sprittle and whirr.

As others copied, she shifted again:

Whoosh-skirr, whoooosh-skirr, Skirr-skirr-skirr-whish,
Whoosh-skirr, whoooosh-skirr, Skirr-skirr-skirr-whish,
Whoosh-skirr, whoooosh-skirr, Skirr-skirr-skirr-whish.

More drawn in, she sang:

Splosh and rattle, splosh and spit,
Splosh and rattle, splosh and spit,
Splosh and rattle, splosh and spit.

'Shout with me, sisters!'

Crash and roar, we won't be contained.
Crash and roar, we can't be restrained.
Crash and roar, wildness regained.

The women rose, their voices in harmony,
a mystical cacophony, a sea-noise shanty.
They danced round the bonfire relentlessly

until flames became embers. Women lost
                    in rhythm.
A breaking dawn, a deserted shore,

a red stone circle upon the shingle.
'I didn't tell of my ribbons,'
the woman said sadly. She untied them

from her hair, found there were three –
Marina's ribbon of marled velvet,
Luna's spun as delicate lace

and a third of fine linen
            woven in russet.
                        'Hertha?'

That's my name, so don't be overusing it.
The woman turned, no-one was there
but the wind carried whispers:

Homebound or onward is your choice, journey-woman.
Know who you were, who you are and who you may become.
A cord of three ribbons is not easily broken.

Luna

                Marina

                                Hertha

wax and wane

                wildish ways

                            times and seasons

        ~   ~   ~

Blessing

May the road you walk be edged with scallops.
May you be kept from poverty's pincers.
May you winkle out from stormy waters,
all your whelks heal without a scar.
And until we meet again
may God grow your grit within an oyster shell.

Acknowledgements

Little Blue Hut emerged from a residency at a beach hut on Tankerton Slopes, Whitstable, Kent. I am grateful for Creative Canterbury of Canterbury City Council for providing six weeks for me to 'stand and stare'. Several of these poems have appeared in magazines and anthologies. Thanks go to the editors of *Sarasvati, South, Poetic Licence, Keystone Anthology* and *Canterbury Festival Poet of the Year Anthology, 2012* for giving them space. I would also like to thank the members of the Bellyful poetry group and Jeremy Langrish (find them as *The OtherWise)* for their constant poetry encouragement.